Make America Great Redefined

Saving A sick Nation From Economy Collapse

By Louis Asare

Dedication

This books is affectionately dedicated to my beloved wife Annan Felicia Marvelous whose life and presence has been a great source of inspiration to me during the most important and difficult moments of my life.

Acknowledgements

I wish to express my sincere gratitude to the following people for their immense contribution to my life toward the delivery of this book:

My precious family who have not stopped believing in me and supporting me in all facets of life till now: Felicia, Reinhardrina, Salomey, Perfect, Rachael, Barnes, Randolph and George for being there to counsel and guide me for the realization of this material.

Special thanks also to Frederick Agyekum, Jemimah Antwiwaa, Alberta Pra, Darko Maxwell, George Nsarko, Mantey Larbi Justice and James Mensah.

Appreciation to all members of the publishing team for your great and contributions.

I say God bless you all and keep shining.

Table of Content

Chapter 1

The Benefits Of The Tax Cut Explained

The tax cuts have been a very contentious issue between Republicans and Democrats for years without end, with much discussions being held over its impact on the economy and each social class in the United States. With the Trump's tax bill passed a little less than a year ago, this argument has intensified. Nevertheless, despite the fact that the economy is now prosperous, many detractors or critics continue to contend against the potential benefits of the tax bill and tax cuts in general, some of the critics of the bill believes that these cuts have done more harm than good to the economy. Now to disrepute these claims, let's take a look at some successful tax cut that we have experienced in this nation.

Subsequent to the regime of the Reagan Administration, there was an emergency energy crisis that the Carter government was incapable of solve, thereby causing a serious downturn in the U.S. economy. When it came to economic growth, Reagan encouraged enormous tax cuts and unobstructed free trade (Reaganomics); which in return brought about massive economic success to the country. A combination of Reagan's governance and Reaganomics, by the end of his second term of office, inflation values were lowered to 4% and the unemployment rate was under 6%, and lastly the great economic recession ended.

Furthermore, in history, the Reagan administration has been described as the second-largest job creator government in the country, (Bill Clinton was the first). Reagan's government added about 16.5 million sustainable jobs during his eight-year term. Additionally, throughout Reagan's tenure, the annual growth rate of GDP was projected at a compound rate of 3.6% by the department of commerce when compared to the 2.7% growth rate recorded during the preceding eight years that followed it.

In fact, many families benefitted from Reagan's massive economic policies, with "median family income overwhelmingly growing by $4,492 during the Reagan period. When compared to the last eight years of the president Obama administration, median family income only increased by $1,270 of the last eight years." Under Reagan, the economy saw one of the longest and resilient periods of prosperity in American history, hence proving that tax cuts tremendously helped the economy and the people.

President Trump signed the Tax Cuts and Jobs Act on December 27, 2017. Many opponents understanding of the bill is that, the policy will not help the middle-class of workers in the country. They have warned that the bill will essentially harm the economy more than benefitting it. However, a thorough analysis of the bill reveals that, this is not true. The Trump's tax bill is set to help families, the child tax credit alone is doubling to about $2,000, this is going to help millions of American families throughout the country.

According to the latest Internal Revenue Service (IRS) data, more than 22 million Americans have used the child tax credit in the year 2015.

Moreover, many opponents of the policy have declared that the maximum corporate tax rate was reduced from 35 percent to 21 percent, by maintaining that corporations and companies will only use this superfluous money to increase stock dividends, that will not help the middle-class generally.

Conversely, this is not the case. Though companies did increase stock dividends, that is not the main way that corporations, businesses and companies spent their extra money. Actually, most corporations gave back to their employees. For instance, large banking corporations or companies declared that they were raising their minimum wage from $12 to $15 for all employees in the sector and benevolent gave $1,000 special bonus to more than 13,500 employees, precisely because of the tax cut. For example, another company, Comcast, has pledged to give $1,000 bonuses to 100,000 non-executive employees. Furthermore, AT&T has done something similar by giving $1,000 bonuses to 200,000 of its employees.

In fact, these cases are very common, for the reason that more than four million people are being paid bonuses, benefit growths and higher wages are coming from hundreds of companies operating in the country. This sums up to some $4 billion paid back into the pockets of the working class people and their families. Demonstrating how extensive this bill has had on the middle and working classes in the country.

Moreover, according to the Tax Foundation's progression model, their model estimates or projects that about 215,000 new full-time jobs that are well paying will be created before the end of the year 2018. These activities are happening as a result of the latest tax bill, thereby explaining how tax cuts are helping the middle and working class group of people in the country. In fact, many people have received substantial bonuses and wage rises, thereby enabling them to live more happily, comfortably and better their quality of life. Again, there are more job openings, providing people with more varieties in discovering their career path.

Besides the fact that the bill has helped the middle-class workers and their families, let's examine the bill's effects on the economy so far. For the first time in some years, the economy grew at a rate of 4.1 percent rate in the second quarter of the year, the best quarterly showing since 2014. Talking about consumer spending, that was not left out, it rose by 4% percent in the spring quarter of 2018, that is the biggest increase since 2014. Additionally, hiring speeds are rapidly increasing, with American manufacturing companies and factories hiring employees at their fastest rate in two decades. The unemployment rate has lowered to 3.7 percent in September, its lowest level since 1969, this is showing a strong labor market in the country meaning that the economy is firing on all cylinders. In fact, tax cuts have ushered in strong economic performance for the United States of America thereby showing the bill's rewarding benefits to the citizens of the United States.

Through the Reagan government previously illustrated tax cuts' past success, and the Trump government is now experiencing economic prosperity, the conclusion about tax cuts is clear: by cutting taxes the United States of America will reap in the overabundance of benefits. In fact, many detractors will continue to condemn this bill, nevertheless, it is flawless that this bill and tax cuts in general changes lives and the economy for the better. For example, a common talking point among Democrats is the issue of the tax cut bill as the mid-term elections lingers. It is practically like they're spreading "fake news" to the voters or somewhat.

The fact is this, a new report shows that average American employees are benefiting not exclusively by having their incomes increased by tax cuts, but by having better benefit-packages, too. When presidents of the main political parties have cut taxes over the last 100 years, economic prosperity times have followed. And this happens not just some of the time, but all of the time and this is what we are seeing happening now.

In fact, there is no question about that the fact that American workers are having it better today than they did two years ago. Their salaries are higher now than before. They are receiving heavy bonuses, and to some workers this is the first time they are experiencing such benefits. American workers are receiving better, diverse and heavy benefit packages than ever before.

Chapter 2

Modernized Education Is The Key To The Future

The United States of America has performed very well in terms of the development of education in the world. The government of the United States enhanced the future of the world by leveraging the tools of quality education to the advantage of our economy. As a result of well-developed educational policies and pragmatic efforts, the country has emerged as one of the most important economy of the world. This is partly due to the vision maintained by the various government and leaders of this country over some decades. The American age of the world came into existence simply because we utilized science, technology and innovation.

In recent times, the national boards for scientific and academic, studies in this country have published a series of report that sends signals about the future of this nation. As part of the report the National board for scientific and Academies has disclosed that the United States of America is gradually losing its edge in the fields of Automation and robotics, Biological sciences and Medicine, Engineering and the fields of the sciences. The paper noted that, the very pillars that have kept this nation for several years are beginning to crumble at the times when we need them most.

In fact, the scientific and the technical foundation or building blocks of our nation are beginning to fade or erode at a more challenging time. For, instance, the leadership of our technical and scientific education is gradually falling and our output in the fields of the sciences, engineering and medicine is declining at the point where other nations in the world are also emerging.

This means that other countries are becoming visionary after studying the policies of the United States of America whiles at the same time, the United States of America is becoming complacent and beginning to ignore and lose sight of how this nation became great.

So, we are entering a critical point in the history of this nation. Some of the leading politicians of our country are not even aware of the challenges confronting our nation presently. This could potentially mean that, the future leaders of this country should also become aware of the problem so that we can manage it well.

As at now, our country is actually leading the world in terms of how we do business and the investment our government is making in education and other sectors. Notwithstanding, it is like, we are going to set up ourselves for long term failure in the very near future because other emerging countries are investing aggressively in education and technology.

A senior analyst at the united states of American treasury by name Mr. Henry Paulson has predicted from one of the reports submitted by a think tank group that by year (2045-2050) China and India will supplant the United States of America as the most important economy of the world.

The size of the Chinese and the Indian population gives them access to a wide range of human resources that the United States will not be able to match in the near future. At time where both China and India are rising in their confidence level for global leadership, the population of the United States of America is gradually slowing.

So, these scenarios will serve as indicators that without drastic policy implementation, the United States of America will be toppled by India and China. This will mean an end to the American era and age and many generations of Americans will regret how our country has lost global power and impact at the world stage.

So, there is room for great work with effective planning, our government should reprioritize science and technology as we move into the future. Our ability to adapt to the changing trends of the educational system and the willingness of our people to study science and technology courses will determine the fortunes of our nation before the middle of the twenty first century. We must all get on board that is both the private sector and the public sector of this country to help our government to steer the affairs of this country in the right direction.

Another major problem that this country is facing is its inability to attract intelligent and brilliant students. This was one of the factors that have accounted for the growth of our economy. For several decades, our country was a spot on the globe where many brilliant and intelligent students from foreign countries were attracted to study in this country and afterwards progressed to work in some of the most important companies of this country.

In fact, according to the managers of the hedge fund, many of them are quoting figures that, about twenty-five percent of Americans wealth belongs to people who have entered America to study and later worked in this country. For example, in the field of science and technology we have figures that suggest that where ever significant innovations were made in America there were foreign brains behind it.

Unlike in the by gone days, our country is no longer attracting foreign students. The output of students from the technical and scientific and innovative studies in the country is now on the decline. For example, the number of students who graduated from all American technical institutions and universities was a little over seventy thousand graduates and this is way below that of other countries in the world. It's is on record that China and Japan alone are graduating over nine hundred and fifty thousand (950,000) students annually.

As if this information is not enough, we are informed that the Indian government has also developed an educational system that is very close to that of the American Standard. Currently, India alone graduates more than one million engineering students not to talk about the other sectors. So, these countries are going to rise in the future with proper planning and investment and America may slide to a lower position if care is not taken.

The most recent report conducted by the United Nations on the most industrialized nations on the globe reveals that the current direction of this country is not so bleak and therefore, if government will continue to focus on the best cutting-edge technology, science and innovation we may be reserved with a place in the globalized world.

The world has actually changed at a very fast pace in the twenty first century as a result of globalization. In spite of these changes our country is still having dominance in the world. The indicators published by the United Nations on the most industrialized nations states that the United States of America is currently the leading producers of world economic output.

America contributes about thirty percent of global output and this is a significant improvement of the country over the previous decades. It means that our country has improved over the past few years. The report also ranks the United States of America as the best country in terms of technological innovation. The country is also leading with the first position on the ranking in corporate research and development of systems. The United States of America is also ranked as the best country that invests much money into its research institutions.

Chapter 3

Danger Of Rising Health Care Cost For Workers

Health care has been one of the most important Pillars of our nation. The health of our people has been of a serious concern to our government. As part of efforts by the government, the national insurance health care scheme had been developed. The government has made it easy for people to enroll on the insurance scheme. With this policy, companies and individuals alike will be able to enjoy affordable health care in our country.

However due to political changes, our country's health care policy has changed dramatically and it is now affecting us negatively. In our country, we have two main types of health care subscribers. The first group involves users who are self-employed and the second group is employer provided health insurance. Our country has seen a surge in the amount that we pay for health care in our nation. For example, the health insurance premiums that companies or employers pay for their employees has surged dramatically by about sixty percent since the first decade of the twenty first century. As a result of this, many people and employers are finding it difficult to pay their health insurance premiums.

In fact, what I mean to say is that, the cost of health care in America from the year two thousand and one to the year two thousand and sixteen have increased astronomically to about sixty percent of what we would have been paying back in the year two thousand.

Now, we can understand from common sense that health care is one of the most important priorities of every living thing. We must be able to access quality and affordable health care with a little cost. But this is not the present situation in America. Health care bills have increased sharply and it is beginning to weigh heavily on individuals and companies that pay for the health insurance premium of their employees. The problem we are beginning to face in this country is that as the cost of health care continues to increase there is the probability that the rate of employment levels will decrease as companies and government will try to reduce cost by freezing employments.

Another challenging effect of the risen health care cost is that some companies have adapted to this situation by changing the work conditions of employees. This will mean that full time employment positions can be changed to part time employment position in cases where the employer will not be compelled by law to pay for the health insurance cost of the employees. For example, another paper that we have investigated closely on this subject reveal that when the cost of health care increase by ten percent, it takes a toll on wages. This means that wages will decrease by about three percent in real time. This is a difficult situation that we now find ourselves in and the future is even uncertain about the future health care system.

In our county today, employees who earn lower wages are exposed to the highest risk of not getting the benefits of their employers paying for their health care cost. In recent times, I have been observed that employers find it very difficult to pay for the health insurance cost of employees whose wages is very insignificant around the ten-dollar region. This therefore will imply that the employer can choose to terminate the employment of this low wage employees as a way to offset the cost associated with the rising Health care.

So, with these indicators, we will know that many more working American workers who receive lower wages would likely lose their health insurance coverage by the employer. Again, I would like to say that, when there is a ten percent increment in health care cost then there is a corresponding probability that employers will withdraw the health insurance coverage of low wage-earning employees.

Presently, there is a problem with the cost of health insurance premiums in our country. We have seen this becoming a heavily contested issue in the presidential elections lately. Some of our politicians are of the view that the cost of health care in America is becoming too expensive for many families and companies when compared with other industrialized nations. So, it is an issue of national interest to all the politicians.

These politicians should see through the lenses of the average American employee who is exposed to the risk of losing health insurance as the cost of health care continue to surge. It's like the rising cost of health care has also played a key role in one of the reasons why American jobs are outsourced to overseas countries where health care is cheaper. Even some Americans are beginning to appreciate health tourism as they travel to other countries to receive affordable health care at the cost of the expensive American health care system.

Interestingly, as the cost of health insurance premiums continue to rise very high in less than two decades, we have not seen a corresponding increment in the gross domestic output of our country. This simply means that the cost of health care is rising with imbalanced effect on the nation.

So, this means that we are going to pay higher health cost whiles our earnings remain relatively low. With this system, we are going to see the resources of many companies and families drained as the gains in their earnings will be offset by the extra cost on health care. For example, the cost of health care in other industrialized countries like Germany, and Japan has revealed that over the same period with America, the cost of health care in America has gone beyond these countries.

Now, talking about American health care in details, the records point to the fact that from the year two thousand and ten (2010) the American government spends almost about twenty percent of the nation's gross domestic product (GDP) on health care alone. This is a staggering amount as this will account for several billions of dollars annually. Maybe we can say that the rising cost of health care in America is partly due to the fact that our health care system pioneered the use of advanced health care technology in the world. So, in our country here, we are receiving advanced imaging systems that are used for our diagnostic testing.

The use of technology in our medical facilities has increased drastically yet the impact on our economy is less. For example, when our country is compared to the best twenty countries that earn good income. The United States of America was ranked as the nineteenth country on the index of twenty countries. In spite of the investment made on health care by the government, the life expectancy of an average American citizen is just one year better than it was about two decades ago. This is an indicator that suggests to us that our investment in health has not had enough impact on our lives.

Chapter 4

The Government Should Invest In Cutting Edge Cyber Infrastructure.

It is being a short while since the first computer was manufactured here in the United States of America. The computer industry has revolutionized within four decades and in the world today a new order of the future is being chartered. Computers have become the core structure for the fundamentals of our economy and industry sector. Almost everything today is being controlled by computer systems in one way or the other. The world is now heading towards the information and digital age where everything is going to be controlled by computer and data and communication driven system.

The United States of America was once a key player or leader in the deployment of computer systems, data and communication equipment and sometimes the integration of these systems with satellite technologies for advanced operations in the country. The world was once following after the leadership of America but political uncertainties and policies have compelled other countries to project themselves as the new leaders of the world.

The government of the Republic of India is embarking on the policy of creating a digital India and that is going to transform India into a key world leader in the years to come. This is a new policy recently approved by the Parliament of India and the prime minister of the Republic. They have agreed to invest heavily and hugely in this sector because they want the country to rise to become a key world player and leader in the years to come. This is a measure the Indian government is adopting to follow the lead of the Chinese government and economy.

The United States of America was one of the largest investors in satellite and telecommunication infrastructure and for several years served as the leader in the deployment of supercomputers. But the investment of our nation has changed with many of our government investing more money in building warships and nuclear weapons. The people's republic of China has gradually toppled the United States of America as the country that has more supercomputers and besides that achievement, the three fastest supercomputers are currently located in China. This is a time the United State needs to rise to counter the emergence of other nations. But the unfortunate thing is that, the leadership of the United States doesn't seem concerned about the direction of the future of this nation.

The nation appears to be confused on the path to embark on for the cyber technology for this country. The three fastest supercomputers are in presently located in China and the Chinese government has hinted that their next generation of Exascale supercomputers will be available for testing by the middle of the year two thousand and seventeen.

This is the future of supercomputing in the world and this is an indication of the countries that wants to become the leaders of the World economy in the years to come. The United States has been very slow and will likely not be able to close the gap between China and other fast emerging Asian countries. Indeed, the country has come to a point where we need to focus our attention on the future of the role our county will play in the years ahead.

We have come to a point in time where the national infrastructure of the country is gradually coming under attack or threat. We have seen many of our international companies coming under threat from cyber-attacks from China, North Korea and Russia. These attacks have led to the loss of intellectual properties of our companies to other countries. As if this not enough, the United States government came under the worst form of attacks when the presidential campaign of the United States was swayed by hackers.

This case is currently going through investigation in the United States of America Senate house. These cases and scenarios mentioned above should serves as indicators that the country should adopt a new set of policies that will enhance the investment of government on critical cyber infrastructure.

The critical infrastructure of the United States like water supply systems, pipelines systems, electrical power grids, nuclear weapons and nuclear station, airplane control systems, train control systems and national hospital computers are all reliant on computer network and satellite technologies to operate. These means that a national cyber-attack can expose the nation to serious dangers.

Let us assume no hackers have managed to take control of the systems that controls nuclear weapons in the country. This will be serious threat to life and property in this country. Again, if hackers are able to gain control of water treatment systems that will be dangerous to the nation as the purification process of the water can be manipulated to cause poisoning to consumers. The dangers are just enormous and our country and politicians should not stand in the midst of these challenges unconcerned.

To protect the critical cyber infrastructures of the United States of America, the government will have to perform a twofold operation. The government should reform the education system to include computing technology as part of the fundamental course of studies. For several decades, the educational system of the United States has been centered on subjects like, history, mathematics, science and arts.

Even when government intends to reform the educational sector, usually the reforms are carried out slowing and sometimes not properly monitored to ensure that the intention of government is achieved. Secondly, the government should ensure that more human resource personnel should be trained to manage the cyber infrastructure of the country.

This is indeed a necessity, for example, a recent survey conducted by Google on the teaching of computing courses in the United States of America revealed that the United States is gradually losing holds on the future. The survey conducted on students shows that about thirty percent (30%) of

American students don't have access to well-resourced computer laboratories. The survey also revealed that there are about fifteen percent (15%) of American students do not have access to computer laboratories in their school.

This is a message to the government that the nation should once again invest heavily in the development or training of people for the administration of cyber systems. This is a critical point of the country because other countries are gradually beginning to overtake the United States in terms of how computer systems are being used.

The commerce department of the United States of America published in one of their articles last year that there are about three hundred thousand various vacancies in the fields of cyber technology. The educational system of the United State of America is not able to supply enough human resource personnel to occupy all the job vacancies in the country.

This should inform the planning of the government because we now depend on countries like India and Japan for well-trained computer experts who come to manned the cyber infrastructure of our country. The United States of America needs to be serious and this will happen when government lays emphasis on the educational system and ensures that more American citizens are trained to give our people the opportunity to work in various capacities for the nation. The government needs to act and now is the time.

The threat of cyber-attacks has come to stay in this country and other parts of the World; we need to get the state of the art technology in place to help in protecting the critical infrastructure of this country. The country should not be look back or turned back, we need to counter the threats and face the future with courage and hope. We have been the leader of the World and if we will recompense ourselves, we will be able to lead the world again. We need to invest in cyber infrastructure so that our systems will be able to counter the threats of hackers on the country.

Chapter 5

The Nation Should Invest In Renewable Energy.

The United States of America is currently the second largest emitter of carbon monoxide gas in the world. Only seconds to the people's Republic of China. The systems of the country have heavily depended on crude oil and other hydrocarbons for a long time to provide power and energy for the industry and economic sectors of the nation. We are currently getting to a point where the world is equally shifting away from carbon energy to renewable energy.

The nations are gradually uniting their efforts in attempt to drastically cut down on the levels of carbon emissions. On the 26th day of May, 2017, several countries from all the continent of the world have gathered to signed up their compliance to the landmark Paris climate agreement, a move that will compel all the nations to combat and curb the emissions of carbon gases by a certain time.

Unfortunately, the United States of America failed to signed on to the Paris climate agreement and the United States has officially withdrawn from the agreement that was championed by the former president of America by name Barack Obama. The United States has actually Shed its leadership roles as the leader of the nations and economies of the world. Therefore, the vacuum must be occupied by someone who is prepared to lead the world to the next level. So, the leaders of these countries like China or India will potentially occupy the position of the United States. This is a wrong step the president has taken and almost all the continents of the world have angrily reacted in disbelief to the future direction of America.

In fact, if this is the "make America great again" that was promised by the President of the United States of America, then American voters should reconsider their choices in the next presidential campaign. The president is actually going to reset the status of the United States of America and for years to come, the unborn generation and the younger generation of Americans will live with the failures of this government in memory. I am saying this because, the government of the European nations and other countries that once followed the leadership of the United States are now losing the trust and confidence they once reposed on America. As a result of this, we are going to see global alliances changed and the isolation of the United States will rather hurt the economy.

In the face of all this, the United States of America has ignored the advice of the international community and the government is deciding to go solo on this issue. So, we will see the country increase its consumption of coal and crude oil related products. The United States has a huge reliance on crude related products. However, during the times of President Barack Obama, he wanted to protect natural resources like rivers and the climates and therefore, he enacted stringent rules and regulations for the environmental protection agency.

The new president of America Donald Trump has gutted the policies of the United States of America on climate and environment and he intends to increase the production of coal and crude products in the country.

The United States is a huge consumer of carbon and coal related products in the world. The American issue on energy has two parts. America produces shale crude oil and the current output level of the United State exceeds that of Saudi Arabia. But do you know something; the United States does not consume the crude oil produced in this country. The crude oil is usually exported to other countries. The United not does not consume much of the shale crude oil because it is said that the shale crude oil doesn't contain much Sulphur, therefore it is not good for the American energy sector.

In the month of March two thousand and seventeen (2017) the trade deficit of the United States increased largely due to huge import of petroleum products from Saudi Arabia and other gulf states. The nation has become heavily dependent on petroleum products and government does not appear to be finding alternatives that will help reduce the nation's dependence on crude related products. The nation's over reliance on petroleum products for a long time is currently responsible for the changes that are occurring in the oceans and climates. Besides these external damages to the environment, the government of America has incurred huge cost as a result of spending billions of dollars in importing crude from Gulf States and Saudi Arabia.

Now, China is gradually emerging as the new leader of clean energy as they have defined the most stringent rules for carbon emissions. The Chinese government is actually building electrical charging stations across the length and breadth of the country. To them, they are compelled because of the high levels of pollution that has been occurring in their nation. As a result of this, China has the most electrically powered cars more than any country in the world. These are some of the indicators that proves that the Chinese are actually looking forward to occupy the imperial position that America is gradually losing hold of.

The impact of carbon emission on the climate and environmental can be so damaging that it will cost hundreds of trillions of dollars to reverse if government doesn't attach important to it. It is a very difficult moment; our nation has seen severe drought and rainfall changes that have affected states like California and other wonderful states. Climatic changes will actually be hard to reverse and this is the reason why government should commit to finding alternative renewable sources of energy. This will include harnessing wind technology, solar technology, ocean current technology and other technologies that generate clean and environmentally friendly energy.

The other danger that the United States should seek to address in this regard is the nations over dependence on foreign crude oil. The United States receives much of her crude oil from Saudi Arabia and other Arab nations. There is a situation that could cause these countries to one day block the supply of petroleum products to the United States of America. The issue is Palestinian and Israeli conflict.

The United States has actually failed to broker a lasting peace deal for almost a half century. The Arab nations are gradually losing confidence in the government of the United States and will retaliate against America in case the American government mishandles those conflicts. The first thing those countries will do against America is to cut the export of crude oil to the United States and secondly, they will not accept the payment for crude oil in dollars or the American currency. Looking at the potential dangers that are currently about to unfold in the next few years because of the political situation in America.

This will mean that the American economy will be strongly and severely hit when the Arabs countries cut the supply of crude oil products to the United States of America as protest for the way the American government handled the Israel and Palestine crisis. This problem is just too glare for anybody to ignore and I am finding it difficult to understand why the government is acting like it is all well for the future of this nation.

I have mentioned earlier in this chapter that the United States of America produces crude oil and refined petroleum products in large quantities. Most of the country's output is exported to other countries and not used here in America. So, the American products are such as refined petroleum products, natural gas and crude oil are exported to other markets and then we import the crude oil and other products that we use in this country from other countries. So, any inconvenience created by the suppliers of crude oil to the United States will have dire consequences on the economy of the United States.

This is a matter of necessity that the America should seriously invest in alternative or renewable energies that will reduce country's dependence on petroleum products. The country needs to invest in alternatives energies. Because the dangers of this country will be too costly to bear if we sit down idle for calamity to strike at our door step.

Chapter 6

The Buy America Act Should Be Enforced Once Again.

After the First World War, America had made contribution to the war and was suffering from economic decline and stagnation. The economic development of the nation at the time compelled the government of the day to implement strategies and policies that will stimulate and cause the economy to grow more. After a brief session of consultation and discussion from the leading policy maker, a decision was reach in the year nineteen thirty-three (1933) during the presidency of Herbert Hoover of the United States of America.

The said president of America signed a series of executive orders in attempt to stimulate the American economy. The Executive orders of the president directed Congress to Draft and enacts the buy America Act into law. The purpose of the law was to promote the manufacturing of finished

Goods in America. This law therefore compelled all citizens to cherish products made in the United States of America. As, a result of the new development, the subsequent governments ensured that America made goods enjoyed premium over foreign made goods that are sold in the country.

The policies actually helped the economy to emerge out of economic crisis toward a path of growth and prosperity. Industries and companies actually emerged as consumers were encouraged to use things made in America.

In fact, around the early nineteen thirties (1930) through to the nineteen seventies (1970's) manufacturing became the major employer in our country before all other sectors. Those days, people were actually taking pride in buying things made in our homeland here. The memories of those good days can still be remembered. It was a pride for American citizens back then because everything you see in your store or in your kitchen was made in the United States of America. The embossment "made in America" caused more consumers to spend on things made in our country. Those were the powerful and the most significantly amazing times in the history of this nation.

This is actually not a new policy in the history of America at all. As far back as the seventeenth century, the then president elect by name George Washington before his swearing in ceremony tried to outline best economic policies that will help him to develop the United States of America from the imperial rule and governance of colonial Britain. As a result of this brainstorming exercise, president George Washington detailed his treasury secret by name Alexander Hamilton to come out of the strategic set of policies that will help American to rise and break the shackles of Britain.

Now, if you have not read about it, I will like to say something little about the trade practices of Britain. The British then operated a trade system that favored "Britain" and "Britain first". This means that if the deals will not favor the British government and business then it is out of consideration.

When the intentions of George Washington and his treasury secretary Alexander Hamilton and Congress were leaked to the British government, the British government responded by cutting all supplies to the United States of America. So, the consequence was many of the Americans to endure life during those days of economic hardship. For example, I understood from my research that, president George Washington could not get a good suit for his swearing in ceremony because Britain had stopped supplying America with fine clothing and machinery.

Fortunately for President George Washington, an American native had also started a fabrics company so they consult the local manufacturer for the suit which the president used for his inauguration ceremony. According to the history archives, I understand that the suit he wore wasn't so great so he later imported some from Britain. This means that the American economy could be locked out if it depended heavily on imports from countries that can be dangerous and treacherous to the development of our nation.

The government of former President George Washington embarked on the initiative of the buy America Act or the American first economic policies. So, around the nineteen thirties, the government wanted to consolidate on the policies that were already on the law books of the country. The act was successful implemented during the time of Herbert Hoover. Indeed, the economy returned to the path of growth and our economy prospered very well. As long as the policy was in force, the United States of America became the largest manufacturing country in the world and many billionaires and millionaires increased in our country.

The neglect of the buy America Act will serve as the destruction of the greatness of the United States of America. Around the nineteen sixties (1960's) and the nineteen seventies (1970), there was the wave of globalism emerging around America and the world as a whole. The term globalism was later revised to be called globalization. Many Americans felt they belong to a global economy and the results of this will not help the United States of America. As a result of the wind of globalization that was spreading in the print media and the digital media, many people wanted the American government to participate fully in globalization.

Around this time, the government of former President Nixon and also former President Ford has actually initiated policies that will allow the United States of America to participate fully in globalization. So, around the nineteen seventies (1970's) to be precise, the then present Ronald Reagan of the United States of America signed executive orders to inform all departments of the United States government that they have the permission to engage fully in buying things from outside the United States of America.

The situation that was begun in the year nineteen seventy-nine (1979) by former President Ronald Reagan will serve as the turning point for the economy of the United States of America.

This development of the new government's move against the established laws that had been used to build the United States of America. This new law will now transform the greatest manufacturing country of the World into the largest buying country in roughly over a period of three decades. Until this disaster, the laws in the books of our country stated that anything that is bought or purchased by any state department or the federal agencies of the government will have to be made or manufactured or sourced out to an American supplier.

The government is a huge buyer and a key driver in terms of spending. It is estimated that the government spends between five percent to eleven percent of the annual budget. When the purchase was sourced from local American supplies that was a boon to the economy and the manufacturing sector.

Since the time when the administration of former President Ronald Reagan authorized the use of special waivers to buy things from outside the country. Almost all the state departments are buying more things from outside America. The impact of this law is now having negative effect on the economy as both the private and public sectors are now buying more from outside America.

Because the country has lagged behind in manufacturing because of preference for foreign made goods, whole industries like the electronic and the clothing sectors have been closed down with jobs now outsourced to other countries. The disastrous effect of the new policies of government has sharply increased the trade deficit of America with other countries. America has become the largest borrower in the world,

No government has actually tried to halt this process and therefore the practice has continued by several administrations and America is now exposed to undue competition that makes it difficult for American companies to compete. The battle can be worn but then, it will be with strong determination. Any government that wants to make America great again will have to restore the buy America Act in full. It is only then that this nation can revive the local manufacturing sector. Yes, the trade deficit can be reduced and the practices can be halted within a short time. It is not good news that our country has transformed from being the largest manufacturer of the World to becoming the largest buyer of finished goods in the world as we see today.

Chapter 7

The High Cost Of Free Trade To Our Nation

The great economies of Britain, the Greek Empire and the Roman Empire operated strict protectionist policies that controlled and protected the development of the countries' or empire's local companies and industry. These countries and empires prospered until they eventually took off the triggers and boom they went down. America is a nation that also started out with strong protectionist principles and the nation became very great. The country became the largest creditor to the world.

Since the advent of free trade around the early nineteen eighties (1980, s) and nineteen nineties (1990). The tables started flipping or turning against the economy of the United States of America. The country would now find itself entangled in a situation where we will be competing with low wage countries. This is going to have a difficult impact on the country because we cannot offer things at such cheaper prices.

So, the low wage countries will outwit America on the free trade playing field. This is the reason why American made goods have actually vanished from the market and stores. This has taken a heavy toll on the industry sectors of the economy. We have seen more job losses in the country presently more than at any time in the history of this country. We are made to understand that the sharp increase in our national trade deficit represents over four million lost jobs. This is not how it supposed to be for our country.

In one single generation, precisely our country has fallen from being the largest creditor of the World to become the largest debtor nation on the earth.

The Asian countries that are now anticipating for free trade all over the world were not even recognized as economic superpowers when American had control over the manufacturing industry. Again, around the (1930's) none of the countries presently promoting free trade all over the world was not having industrialization initiatives. So, these countries gradually learnt about the industrialization principles of the United States.

So, when, they wanted to compete with America at the world stage, these countries adopted or revised the principles of the American economy and that is how they have emerged to compete very closely with our country. In fact, what I am saying is that, countries like Japan, China, South Korea, Taiwan and India all learnt from America.

When America closed her doors to free trade at the world stage around nineteen thirty (1930) until nineteen seventy-nine (1979). The country served as the largest manufacturer of the world. Unfortunately, when the doors were eventually opened to free trade in nineteen eighties (1980's).

The moment the nation step on the pathway to free trade, the greatness of the country began to fall.

The country opened its borders to products made in overseas countries like China, India and Japan where the cost of labor is very low. These countries have now become the biggest manufacturers in the world. These countries have rapidly replaced America as the largest manufacturer in the world in less than one generation. The world has become heavily dependent on Asian countries as suppliers for the supply chain.

In the very few decades ago when American industrialization was at its peak. Almost all our products were made in our country here in places like Michigan, California, Alabama and Connecticut. These were the days our economy boomed and many people became rich and the middle-class level increased in our country. Due to the devastation of free trade on our country, we have become used to layoffs, and our factories have become obsolete and abandoned and those jobs have shifted to overseas countries.

Our country is now standing at the cross road of her greatness and our government should be able to implement good measures and policies to safeguard the country. When jobs have been lost and these jobs have been outsourced to Countries like India, China and South Korea.

These countries are currently experiencing shortage of labor supply to occupy the operational position in factories and companies. Our country is battling with abandoned factories and mass layoffs from the manufacturing sector.

When the United States strictly practiced protectionism, the country emerged as the most industrialized country of the world for almost two hundred years. We are now losing hold of our place at the world stage and China is aggressively pushing the United States of America.

For example, in the year two thousand and nine (2009), there was a shortage of labor supply, a situation that led to the increase in the cost of wages in that country. In our homeland, wage growth has stagnated in our country. China has surpassed the United States on almost all ends when America drop protectionism. Today, free trade has made the rich countries poor and the poorer countries have become richer.

I have been informed that the United States of America is now producing more millionaires than billionaires and has fallen behind with the number of billionaires. For example, China is clipping on America at a faster pace. The number of billionaires is increasing very fast China such that every week a billionaire is produced. This is happening because many manufacturing companies have been established there and the products we consumer or use now comes from China instead of the United States. This is exactly the opposite of how it used to be. Things have changed completely and significantly in the world. We have seen wealth and resources shifting from wealthy countries in the west like the United States of America and Europe to countries like China, Singapore, Japan, India, Vietnam and South Korea among others.

Today when you go to the leading retail stores like Walmart, Amazon, Sears and other major stores. Majority of the products sold in those stores are made outside the United States of America. When these retailers close their working operations or schedules, the single event of clicking or pressing on a computers button will siphon all the monies and distribute them to the various supplies of the imported products.

The consequences of the whole business are that, the more our reliance on foreign made products increases, our local companies and industries are going to suffer and move out of business. There will be more pressure on our government as monies that could have been used on other internal projects are being spent on importing products thereby draining our economy of precious cash.

The sad news about the whole practice is this; we pay dollars to the suppliers of such commodities like machinery, consumables and pharmaceutical products, electronic and crude products. Because we pay in dollars, after all transactions, the money must still return to the American central bank.

Secondly, the dollars cannot be used for majority of transactions in those countries. So, the dollars our retailer companies and other agencies have paid to their foreign suppliers are being used to fund the acquisition of massive infrastructure and investment in America. This is how things are playing out. The government of our nation should act quickly to remedy this development from escalating into something else.

Chapter 8

There Should Be Judicious Regulations For The Inspection Of Manufactured Commodities.

It is not a new thing at all to hear companies' releasing press messages that informs the public to either adhere to caution or return an equipment or machinery to the manufacturer due to problems or errors detected with the products that can cause potential malfunctioning. This is a trend that has occurred in this country and other parts of the world especially the Asian manufacturing hubs.

For example, in the year two thousand and sixteen Guiro Inc. is an American company that is into the manufacturing of unmanned Arial vehicle (UAV). The company detected after they have shipped products to the stores that they detected that the batteries of some drones were not functioning, as a result, they have recalled all the drones and the shares of the company plunged for the rest of the year. We have heard that Ford Motor Company has recalled several thousands of cars as a result of faulty airbags. As if this is not enough, General motors, the mother of American automobile companies also recalled thousands of vehicles and cars because of failure in the braking system of the car.

Whenever, things of this nature occur, the shares of the companies will usually plunge or dip either for that quarter of the financial year or for the whole financial years. This is a trend that has gradually settled over the manufacturing sector of the United States of America. As, the companies have made huge losses through these negligence, other countries have lost confidence in the credibility of the United States of America to produce well tested and durable equipment's. This is actually the time for the government of this nation to revive the regulations that calls for the thorough inspection of finished goods before export to international markets and even for the domestic market.

This country was highly regarded for the production of high quality materials and equipment's in the years gone by. However, the United States of America has rapidly lost this trust and ability as many of the leading firms in America have crushed to their knees because of the negligence that have occurred in the past. For example, I came across a story on the Internet that states that, the government of China and Japan together with other countries from the European Union doesn't trust the credibility of the United States manufacturing sector.

So, just as I have mentioned at other parts of this book, Alexander Hamilton, proposed a long time ago, that the only way the manufacturing sector of the United States will be able to topple and supplant great Britain as the world's best manufacturer then was to ensure that thorough inspection is carried out on finished goods before they are cleared from the company floors to the market.

Today, the laws have been relaxed and the various inspector agencies are not working in the manufacturing sector of our economy as it used to be. The implications of this negligence are seen in the high-profile levels of recalls that we have seen our companies handling in recent times. In spite of the many obstacles confronting the manufacturing sectors, the government can once again streamline efforts to revive and strengthen the qualitative edge of the United States of America. If these measures are adequately implemented, the United States of America will return to its position as leaders in the manufacturing sector.

If the government of the United States of America wants to revamp the manufacturing sector, then the judicious inspection of finished goods should not be considered among the least important measures. All efforts and resources of government should be focused on the implementation of this policy so that government will be able to monitor the manufacturing processes of companies in the country. Look, if the law enforcement agencies will do their work effectively, the American manufacturing sector will once again return to levels of prosperity. This therefore implies that the enforcement of judicious inspection of finished goods is very essential for the success and prosperity of the United States of America. This is doable and the government of America can return the country to the path of industrial excellence.

When the government focuses on judicious inspection of finished goods, this will contribute to prevent frauds or the supply of fake or pirated goods upon consumers at home or foreign countries. This will also help our companies to exporter high-quality products to foreign countries or overseas consumers. This will help our companies to improve the quality of finished products and also protect or preserve the character of the national manufacturers in our country. This country has served as industry leaders of the world for several years and we can still overcome the great gap that we are currently facing now. The country can do well; let our leaders rise up to redirect the country.

Chapter 9

The Raw Materials Of Manufacturers Should Be Exempted From Duty.

The administration of President Donald Trump tried to impose cross border taxes on all products entering the United States when he met with the leaders of the major corporations and companies in the country. Something happened at the meeting that day when president and his economic team floated the idea of imposing tariffs on all imports. There was a mix of reactions at the meeting that afternoon. Some of the companies agreed with the views of the president.

For example, the chief executive of Boeing Inc., proposed that the government should impose taxes on finished goods from other countries entering the American market. The company's director proposed that raw materials should be exempted from taxes and companies should be supported when exporting their products or equipment. They argued that the taxes will make it very effective for American companies to compete with other companies at the world market. This is the protectionist idea of the president and he is seeking to embark on this initiative as a way of reviving the manufacturing sector in the United States of America.

On the other hand, the other companies that attended the meeting opposed the president's initiative of floating taxes around the border. Companies like Amazon, Walmart and General Electric among other multinational American companies argued that floating cross border taxes will be very destructive to the operations of American companies operating in other countries. They argued that there will be retaliatory measures taken by other governments to counter the measures of the American government. The country will be must return to the path of industrial success as it used to be in the past successful years.

During the years of the industrial success of our country, Alexander Hamilton suggested that the government of the United States should exempt critical raw materials that are in very high demand for manufacturing from taxes. This is a policy that will enable our manufacturing companies to get access to raw materials at cheaper prices that make it possible for our companies to compete with manufacturers from other countries.

We are convinced that when the government implements the policy that totally eliminates taxes on the raw materials, our companies will also be able to manufacture finished goods at prices that are low enough for even poorer households to afford. This will increase the competitiveness of our country as one of the key suppliers of finished goods to the world market.

It is in regard to trying to revamp the manufacturing sector of the United States of America that we are working on this book. There is really the need for the government to remove taxes from all the raw materials that enters our country. For example, at the meeting with the president and the leaders of the major companies in America. The managers of large corporations like

General Electric, Boeing Inc., and Lockheed Martin and suggested that the government should progressively work towards removing the taxes on raw materials. The country's industry sector is waiting for some drastic policies that will overhaul and restore competitiveness to the American economy.

This is not a new thing in the history of the United States of America; this policy has been practiced in the United States for so many years. But just as I have said in the past, some of our politicians lost focus on the very fundamental things that have sustained the United States for over two hundred years successful. However, along the line, our leaders lost sight of the benefits of some policies and removed them. Some of these decisions were taken without consultation with the manufacturing sector. The economy needs rapid transformation policies and as our new president is focusing on revival for the manufacturing sector, the president should ensure that the best policies are employed for sustainable development of our companies and industries.

Another important thing about exempting raw materials from taxes is that, foreign companies can even move to invest in the manufacturing sector of the United States of America. The good news for these companies is that they can import raw materials from their country of origin to the United States of America without paying any taxes or duty. This will help the government to stimulate the economic growth of the country. This policy will make the industry sector of America so attractive to other companies from overseas countries.

At the beginning of the year two thousand and fifteen, the Indian government has embarked on the process of clearing all barriers that makes it difficult for foreign companies to operate or invest in India. The result is that; the Indian government has seen many companies investing in the manufacturing sector of India. I was surprised to hear that India has become the fastest growing economy in the world and the amount of direct foreign investment in India for the year two thousand and sixteen (2016) amounted to seventy-nine billion ($79 billion) dollars.

It has been predicted that the Indian economy will surpass that of the United States of America by the year 2050. More recently, the prime minister of India has given invitation to European companies to invest in India. And we have seen many American companies shifting their production to overseas countries.

It will therefore be proper for the government of the United States to implement drastic measures that will eliminate all barriers hindering local and foreign companies from investing in the United States of America. Our country needs to attract many foreign companies to invest in this country. Furthermore, the business climate should be convenient for both local and international American companies to invest here in America. If these measures are judiciously carried out, then our country will be able to survive the heat of the economic storm that will blow up the fortunes of the countries.

Chapter 10

Prohibitions Of The Exportation Of The Materials Of Manufactures.

Majority of the industrialized countries in the Asian sub region depends on other countries for many of the raw commodities and products that are used in those countries. The industry of these countries depends heavily on raw materials from places like Africa or Australia. These countries are able to supply the world with majority of the products that are used in the industry for manufacturing processes.

In the case of the United States of America, thus the country that once served as the major importer of raw materials from the world market. The industry sector has crumpled to all time low and many companies in our country have closed down. We see so many dilapidated factories and machines everywhere. Our people have become used to layoffs. Almost every day a factory is being closed down in our homelands. It is not surprising that President Donald Trump mentioned in his inaugural address that the country is dotted with so many closed down factories in every state and city.

The United States of America has lost so many companies and factories within two decades. For example, we are, made to understand that the United States of America lost about eighty-five thousand factories since China joined the world Trade organization in the years two thousand and one (2001).

This therefore means that the capacity of the nation to serve as the largest importer of raw materials will be dented in very near future. Indeed, in this modern era, especially in this twenty first century, the destiny of this nation is being strangled very hard but our lawmakers need to formulate good policies to correct and rectify these difficult challenges that are almost trying to swallow up our economy.

Now, because our country has lost many factories from the early nineteen eighties (1980's) till date, the United States of America's ability to serve as the importer of raw materials has been weakened with time. This is currently happening because China has toppled and supplanted the United States to become the world's largest manufacturing country of the world. This is actually a difficult time in the history of our nation and we can believe that with policy restructuring, our country will become very prosperous and strong again. The battle is not lost and our government should not give up absolutely on the need to strengthen our economy.

The United States of America has become the largest exporter of iron rod and crude oil and natural gas. If you have followed me closely, you will remember that I said about three decades ago, the United States of America used to be the largest importer of raw materials from the world market. But when the fundamentals of the American industry became weak, we have relinquished that position to China.

We have now become the leading exporter of natural gas and iron ore. The last research I performed before the write-up of this material reveals that the United States currently surpasses Saudi Arabia as the leading producer and exporter of crude oil. This all points to the fact that the basic fundamentals of the industrialization of our country have become weak.

I once spoke to a Chinese man and he shared some wonderful things with me. He told me that, they have a proverb in their settings that says that, the wasted resources are already wasted but drastic measures should be taken to correct the anomaly that caused the losses. This is the situation the United States finds herself now. It has come to the political circles where presidential candidates have spoken about reviving the manufacturing sector of the American economy.

The United States has to learn from the past especially regarding our transition from being the largest creditor of the World to becoming the most indebted country of the world. And, our gradual transition from being the largest importer of raw materials to becoming the largest exporter of raw materials.

The government should now initiate policies that will revive the manufacturing sector of the United States of America. The government should now reduce the export of materials that are very essential for the manufacturing sector. The government should then subsidize the operational activities of companies that seek to invest in the manufacturing sector in the United States.

The manufacturing sectors should be rebranded in a way that will attract more companies to invest in America. When companies move to site their factories in our country, the government should periodically compensate them for their investment. When these measures are in place, the government should then limit the export of precious raw materials that are heavily used in the industrial sectors. The trend of massive export of precious raw materials should be discouraged or stopped by the government so that these materials can be used to supply the needs of the American industrial sector.

When we keep majority of the raw materials in this country, this will enable our companies to gain access to these materials at a cheaper price as the burden of transportation from foreign countries will totally be eliminated from the supply chain. This will also keep the down the price of finished goods at relatively low price. The sectors include agriculture, natural gas, crude oil, precious metals among others.

If done correctly, the United States of America will gradually return to the path of excellence and economic prosperity. This is because; the manufacturing sector has the capability to employ so many people even in spite of automation. For example, we understand that the current trade deficit of the United States represents about four million manufacturing jobs.

You see, if we revive the manufacturing sector, the United States will be become successful and efficient again. With the best measures, our local companies will be able to meet the demands of our local market. This will become a milestone of great achievement in the history of our national manufacturing operations.

We are still expecting the prosperity of our country to be restored to `us; we will not accept anything else. We need to succeed and we need to emerge out of the debt we currently find ourselves in now.

The solution to the problems with our country is the manufacturing sector and if we are able to revive it then we can laugh and relax because our prosperity will bounce back again. We cannot fail and we will not accept failure for this country. We have done it before for over two hundred years with much success. Though we have been negligent at some point in the history of this country but that is not our primary focus now. We will surely overcome these problems and return this nation back to greatness again.

Chapter 11

The Government Should Support Exports

Until the early eighteenth century, the United Kingdom had been the most industrialized country of the world. The possessed majority of the companies around that times and accounted for the largest exports of finished goods to the world. The British government at the time operated a system that helped British companies to export more products whiles discouraging excessive imports of products that can be easily produced in the country. These measures sustained the British economy for several years until the emergence of the United States of America.

So, when the former leaders of the young American nation at that time met to decide the future of the country. Again, in the strategy of Alexander Hamilton the treasury secretary of George Washington suggested that the government should implement a policy that will support the export of products to the world. These measures were actually implemented by the United States of America and the policies have worked so well for about two hundred years in the United States of America.

In spite of the massive success that our country has enjoyed from the good policies that other government have implemented. We have so soon lost sight of our direction. In the name of trying to reduce the national debt, the government of the United States has implemented some policies that compelled the government to cut down incentive policies that once drove the American economy to success.

For instance, when the Second World War ended, Germany was heavily devastated by the effect of the war. So, the Germans embarked on a strategy to industrialized their country and then transform the country into the largest exporting country in the world.

You will be surprised to see what happened afterwards, Germany has become the second largest exporting country in the world. Germany became the first country in the world for the financial year ended two thousand and sixteen (2016) to post the largest trade surplus with other Countries. The trade surplus of Germany surpassed that of China and Japan making it the best trading country in the world. The success of the German economy can be closely tracked down to the policies once pursued by the United States of America suggested by Alexander Hamilton and implemented by George Washington and Congress.

The United States of America should now make a U-turn and look back at other countries that have maintained their focus and let us try to bring ourselves back into the game. This would be possible if our government will be gentle enough to perform the great work that lie ahead of our country. For instance, the United States should emulate the success of countries like Germany, India, Vietnam, Singapore, Taiwan, Japan, Hong Kong, South Korea, and China.

These countries that I have listed above have implemented some specific policies that allow their government to offer incentives to other nations that buys goods manufactured from those countries. The American government can also follow the lead of the above-mentioned countries so that the American government will also offer some incentives to nations that buys American made or manufactured goods. This will help in promoting American made goods in oversea countries. Again, this will help to increase America's presence at the world market place since the country has lagged behind for so long a time.

If you have followed through closely on this subject, most of those countries that I have listed above adopted a reversible value added taxes which the government uses to offset the import and export expenses of business. This reversible value added tax system function as tariffs up to thirty percent and sometimes even beyond that thirty percent. The reversible tax system enables those countries to steadily balance out the cost of export and import.

This is the reason why you see so many German made cars and machinery in the United States of America and other parts of the World. Also, the government of Japan has a similar system and that is the reason why we see a lot of Japanese made cars in the United States of America and sometimes at other parts of the World. And because the American government is currently not providing any incentives for the export of American made goods, that is the reason why we see few American made products in Germany or Japan. The government should stir up the game and try to bring America back into competitiveness.

I still believe that America will not collapse under heavy unsustainable national debt and therefore, one of the key drivers to help in revitalizing the American economy will be a strong industry sector and strong export policies. The government cannot afford to sit unconcerned about the wholes development currently. The mounting debt that America is posting with other countries of the world is just unacceptable.

For example, by the end of the year two thousand and sixteen, American trade deficit with all the countries of the World was hovering around six hundred billion dollars ($600 billion). The trade deficit between America and China stands at around three hundred billion dollars the highest ever in the history of America against a single country. It is currently being estimated by many economists that the trade deficit of America will skyrocket to around nine hundred billion dollars ($900 billion) by the end of the two thousand and seventeen (2017) financial years.

This should be seen as an emergency and therefore government should take drastic measures to bring down the national trade deficit with immediate effects. The United States of America as I said has suffered the impact of globalization more than any other country in the world. As a result of globalization, most of the American companies have either closed down or have moved to cheaper cost producing countries.

The end result is that America has now disappeared from the market place at the world stage. I believe that anyone who lived in America around the nineteen sixties (1960's) and the nineteen seventies (1970's) will tell you that, America has now stepped on the road that is causing the country to sink into debt and potentially a government shutdown in the years to come if government doesn't come out with measure to address this crisis.

When you enter your room and you begin to look around, you will realize that the United States of America has actually disappeared from the global market place. You will realize that almost everything you find in your room or kitchen is either made in China, India, Mexico, South Korea, Germany and Japan. Scarcely will you see made in America again in our county. I should say that there is no way our country will become great again if things continue like this. This is a negative development and hard time for the economy of our country. We need a change and the time is now.

The government should strengthen our import and export bank and make it flexible for our remaining local companies to access credit to export their products to international markets. It is true that the market is already saturated with many countries supplying products to the market. The need to begin from somewhere and with time we will learn the appropriate lessons that will help our economy to respond adequately. I strongly believe that if we can unlock the secrets of the international trade and we can export more to other parts of the World, the United States will recover in a short time.

Chapter 12

The Government Should Impose Protecting Duties On Foreign Articles Which Are The Rivals Of The Domestic Ones Intended To Be Encouraged.

When our country agreed to participate fully in the free trade agreement by joining the world Trade organization. The government has signed so many agreements with many nations currently in the books of the United States; America is having free trade agreement with forty countries and still counting. These agreements have compelled the government of the United States of America to clear all barriers and give foreign companies and foreign articles to get access to the American market. This has made it very easy for cheaper foreign made goods to enter the American market. This therefore makes it very difficult for local American companies to compete.

For example, when the semiconductor industry of the United States was very vibrant American companies did wonderfully well until our markets were opened up for free trade. There was a sudden twist in events. When countries like Singapore and China started producing resources semiconductor chips, the prices of those products were very low that American companies could no longer compete right with foreign made goods in the American market. It is not a wonder that you hardly see an American company in the semiconductor sector that is presently not struggling. This current situation is not going to be healthy for the sustainable development of the industry sector of our economy.

Today, due to the negligence of some American politicians our country has absolutely abandoned whole sectors of the economy. For example, the United States of America has given up important sectors like electronics and textiles. Our country today cannot boast of anything being holistically made in our homeland. We now depend on China for everything from electronics, to clothing and even furniture. When we are exposed to this for a longer time, the future will continue to be bleak and gloomy for this nation. We need to be wise because we cannot rely on a country like China and think that we are safe because they can lock us up or shut us down at their own will. It is therefore necessary that our politicians come into terms with the threats that are presently confronting our country.

The government of the United States can embark on a policy that will impose protecting duties on foreign made articles or products. The benefits of this protecting duty are that, it will make foreign made goods more expensive in America. With this, the local companies will enjoy the advantage of selling products at cheaper prices that will under sell their competitors. This will help our local companies to make profits and increase in their capacity and output. This will be a good way the manufacturing sector of our economy can be set to rebound to the levels of higher production. This is the time for a swift turning and transformation of the country.

Our government should not submit to the pressure of the so called international community by allowing them to dictate the terms of business that rans our country for us. It is really going to be difficult as this process will trigger trade wars and other retaliatory measures from the world. But I can say with confidence that if we will begin to produce everything here in the United States from furniture to computers and clothing, our economy will become the very best as we anticipate. Presently, United States of America is the single largest buying country in the world and any trade war will have dire consequences on the country that initiates it. We can bounce back to the path of prosperity.

It is often said that if everything is to be produced here in the United States of America the cost of items will relatively go up. The indirect benefit we don't see when this issue comes to mind is this. When we begin to manufacture everything here, the prices of goods may go up but there will be much disposal income for people to spend, that will make it possible to offset the increase in the cost of goods. Though prices may go up a little, yet we will not feel the impact at all because money will not be leaving our economy as it is happening now. Presently we are buying a lot of cheap products from foreign markets. We are getting their products at cheaper prices but they are getting our monies. You will not be surprised to see people from China and other Asian countries returning our dollars back to us by buying up many of our stores and companies.

Indeed, we need to actually implement the policy of imposing protecting duties on foreign made products, machinery and articles. When this policy is effectively implemented, this will cause foreign made goods to cost more in America than at other places in the world. The policy will enhance the operational activities of our local manufacturers to enable them to deliver products that will absolutely under sell all foreign competitors here in the United States of America.

This policy will make it very possible for the manufacturing sector of the United States to rebound. Just as the former president Barack Obama said during his presidential campaign and also on the last day of his state address, he said Americans can do it once again, if other countries can learn and come to the point where they are standing on shoulders of the United States, then we can also revise our notes and implement other policies that were once useful to our economy.

Chapter 13

The Facilitating Of The Transportation Of Commodities.

Over the past two decades, the Chinese government had embarked on the project of building large and ultra-fast rail lines to interconnect the major cities in China. This was intended to open up the country for effective supply of equipment's and raw materials through the manufacturing sector of China. This has helped the Chinese people to develop rapidly in less than four decades. Something that has not happened in the history of that country. The availability of roads for the transportation of goods and raw materials has made it very easy for the Chinese to produce goods, equipment's and machineries at a rate that is higher than what other countries are able to do.

Something strange is beginning to happen in China, the president of China called for an international summit and then offered an economic policy that is intended to build ultra-fast train lines from Beijing to the European Union. They wanted to have a train station at London and Berlin that will connect travelers to Beijing or other cities of China in less than three days traveling. The intention of the Chinese government is to allow the country to export more as a way to overcome the industrial overcapacity that is currently happening in the country. This will help China to avoid sea and air transportation as the only way to transport goods from China to other parts of the world.

This is not the story of the United States of America, we heard the president of the United State of America during the presidential election times promising that he will invest heavily in infrastructure such as roads and rail. A moved that will be intended to connect the major cities of America in a special way. The United States of America seems to have neglected some of the important building blocks of this country. A little survey conducted on new road and rail network of the United States of America shows that a lot of American roads and rail lines are in bad shape and conditions. Some of the roads were conducted in the early parts of the twentieth century and have since not seen any significant reconstruction or maintenance since. We cannot even boats of fast or ultra-speed rail lines in the United States of America. The world is heading towards a point of fast transportation and the last time our countries were rated for the easy interconnection of roads, the United States of America came behind countries like Japan, China, Singapore and Germany.

Look at the current indicators, it will mean that the United States of America will still fall back if our governments fail to work on our infrastructure. This is the time the country has been gradually losing sight of important things in the country. At the same time, some of the countries that are gradually competing with the United State are gathering pace and momentum to face the future adequately. These countries will surely rise and if we still don't learn from our mistakes, the greatness of the nation will slump and stagnate until the relevance of the nation is no longer valued at the International stage.

To move the country forward for steady development, the United States government should investment massively in the construction of twenty first century roads and rails. The availability of well-built and interconnected roads and rail lines will make it possible for the movement of commodities within the manufacturing sector of the United States of America. This will make it easy for suppliers and manufacturer to work together at faster time rates that will increase the competitiveness of the manufacturing sector.

The availability of roads, rails, air and sea transport are factors that are important to maintain good relations with the manufacturing sector of the economy. For example, the transportation system of the United Kingdom was constructively designed to help manufacturers of and other key sectors of the British economy. This means that the United States of America will not be exempted from the need to enhanced the transportation facility of the of our country. Indeed, the United States of America is in a position where we need the coordinated facilitation of transportation in this country.

The government of the United States of America should try very hard to construct standard roads throughout all the industrial sectors of the country. The roads and rail networks should be opened up by the government so that the facilitation of the transportation of goods will be easy for the industry sector of our economy.

In fact, government should give attention to the construction of efficient transportation systems because the world has changed and other countries are progressively and aggressively working to break up the imperial position of our country. If the government of the United States fails to act now, we will harvest the results of our in-action and the nation will lose out in the long run.

During the early years of human development, the systems of transportation were rivers and canoes for the movement of goods from one point to another. Also, animals were some used as carriage to move goods from one place to another or sometimes from one big town to a city. It was after several years that modern systems of transportation have been invented. In this present hour, the systems have changed and our country needs to works aggressively to retain our position as one of the planned countries in the world.

In a country like the United States of America where manufacturing has played some significant roles in the economic success of our economy. We can remember that government implemented the construction of roads and rails and other systems that have enabled our country to lead the world for several decades. However, the United States of America has come to a point where others countries have studied and analyzed the forces behind the economic success of the United States and have been working aggressively to overcome the United States of America.

We cannot afford to be sleeping or sitting idle now, by both politicians and other members of the American society. Many countries have united their focus and have come very close to overtaking the position and status of the United States of America. It is estimated that the ambition of the Chinese government and the Chinese people will make China to supplant the United States of America as the most influential and important economy of the world. Besides, China, the world banks economic teams has also forecasted that India will also emerge to the global stage by the year two thousand and fifty (2050).

Chapter 14

The Government Should Protect Small Businesses In America

The United States of America has the record of creating large companies and corporations over the past centuries. The tables have suddenly flipped in the last thirty years to date and businesses and companies have actually struggled in this country. Many of the companies that were once doing very well in the semiconductor industry have all collapsed leaving only a few in this country. This has happened to the other sectors such as clothing, electronics, furniture and even automobile sectors. This therefore makes it necessary for the United States government to now focus on small businesses that have actually gained steam and momentum in recent years.

The last survey conducted by the department of small business administration in the year two thousand and fourteen (2014), there were about twenty-nine million (29 million) smaller businesses operating in the United States of America currently. It is on record that these small businesses and companies employs about fifty-nine million (59 million) employees, according to the institution that conducts assessment on U.S. Small Businesses.

The owners of these businesses have added to the economy by becoming responsible for creating new jobs and hiring employees throughout the length and breadth of the country. These small businesses are actually providing reliable source of income for both new and existing employees in these small companies. Again, these small businesses have actually played a vital role in supporting the families of employees to pay for healthcare cost and other benefits.

The interesting thing about these smaller businesses is that, they are spanning through broader industries in the manufacturing and non-manufacturing sectors of the economy. The tireless efforts and contributions of these small businesses have helped the government to reduce the rate of unemployment in the country. In fact, it is estimated that during first three quarters of two thousand and fifteen (2015), small businesses added almost one million and five hundred thousand (1.5 million) jobs

Currently, there are about forty percent of businesses that employs a minimum of fifty people. This actually, means that small businesses are working very hard to keep the economy of the United States floating and therefore government should pay attention to these sectors with immediate effect.

Following the poor performance of large companies or corporations in recent history, it is becoming appropriate for people who have wealth to invest in small businesses. It is quite difficult to start some small businesses in the United State but it has become a necessity. Sometimes, it is so difficult and challenging to think about getting off the ground to a successful start.

When you have even made up your mind to invest in small businesses, this is the beginning of the challenge among others that investors will face. Notwithstanding, buying all the machinery and assembling all the necessary resources into a fully functional system is not just easy. But this is the twist of event and we must accept the challenge in good faith.

The American economy has actually lost steaming in recent years and the country's ability to produce billionaires has gradually fizzled out. Today, china is producing more billionaire's whiles America is now producing more millionaires. So, the government should strategically support small business owners in the nation to overcome the economic threat that challenges their existence.

So, when investors have actually organized themselves by putting the necessary resources in place such as office apartment, equipment, Web servers and websites and email host among other things. The moment these initial preparatory measures are put in place. The owners of these small businesses will need the financial support and insurance mechanisms that will help them to secure their investments from failing during difficult times in the financial sector.

The revenue levels for small businesses in America that employs a little over one hundred people is estimated to be around three million and seven hundred thousand dollars ($3.7 million). Now, for typically small a business that employs less than one hundred people, the average revenue is sometimes around one million dollars ($1000000) per annum. Sometimes, these companies incur huge debts or losses that can even threatened the existence of these small businesses. Therefore, wisdom demands that the laws should be made very flexible for small businesses or companies to also get access to insurance coverage.

As a matter of necessity, we need to actually help these smaller businesses to grow and at the same time keeping resources protected. I would like to emphasize on this fact that Insurance for small businesses is a necessity. The challenge with this insurance schemes is that, some of the insurance policies are often not customized enough to meet the needs of smaller business investors. This is a difficulty to some people who have invested millions of dollars in small companies that stands the risk of failing due to current economic challenges. These companies have actually generated stable income for people in the country and government should include them in key decision-making processes.

In recent years, we are seeing more small businesses signing up for more insurance schemes and this is commendable. The availability of insurance schemes will make it possible for small businesses to get a financial cover that will actually protect them against shocks. One wonderful thing I have observed is that the small businesses are aggressively signing up and insurance services are beginning to boom in the country.

In fact, we are currently seeing growth rate around double digits and is good news for the economy. So, if we are to ensure credible and sustainable growth of our small businesses, then there must be available tools and resources that will adequately serve the needs of our companies. We must therefore be committed to the sustainability of insurance offering to our small businesses.

Chapter 15

The Government Should Use Stiff Tariffs Measures to Protect American Companies from unwanted competition from outside.

The era of free trade between our country and others countries has actually benefitted some countries at the expense of the United States of America. For example, a recent report published by the department of commerce revealed that between the periods of two thousand and one (2001) to the year two thousand and fifteen (2015) the United States has lost over eighty-five thousand factories (85000). It means that within a period of two decades about eighty-five to ninety thousand factories have been closed down and those jobs have been outsourced to overseas countries and those products are imported back to America freely.

From the research, I have conducted on this subject in my preparation for this book, I have realized that this free trade has actually done more harm to American workers and the economy than good. Our economy is now falling apart as the mounting level of national debt has skyrocketed beyond hundreds of percent of our gross domestic product (GDP) output. American workers are no longer secure on their positions at the workplace as layoff have increased to the point that many leave at risk of losing their jobs.

The threat alone is enough to cause mental and health problems for our people. This is where politics and the oversight of our government have brought the country to. Some years ago, the world's largest manufacturer has suddenly transformed into the largest buyer of the world.

The battle is not completely lost yet as government can adjust the policies and restructure the directions of this nation. We can do well because our country has performed well in the past. We have learnt from history that our country once maintained a stiff tariff mechanism on all products that entered our country through our borders from foreign countries. This is not a new thing because it has been practice in our country here for over two hundred years successfully.

Now, wisdom teaches that, the fundamental principles and ideologies that promoted the development and success of the nation should not be neglected. We cannot afford to sit down unconcerned because history will judge us and our younger generations and descendants will grieve over our in actions that have contributed to the loss of the greatness of this great nation.

I understand that there is a lot of pressure on the government from other countries forcing the government to drop restrictions and tariffs so that there will be a level playing field for all.

Indeed, it is a good idea but some countries are equally manipulating their currencies to take undue advantage of the United States. Because the dollar is being used as the world reserved currency, the government of the United

States has little control of the value of the dollar. This therefore, poses a serious head wind for our economy and business at the expense of the other nations.

The battle is not lost yet, during the presidential campaign for the two thousand and sixteen (2016) election year. The then presidential candidate Donald J. Trump now the president of the United States of America promised to withdraw the United States from all free trade deals that the country has signed.

This is not a new thing in the history of this prosperous nation. It is just a call to return the nation to the pillars that sustained the country for over two hundred years with success stories in business. The president should be urged to carry out with the plan he has promised of withdrawing from all the free trade deals like the North Atlantic Free Trade Agreement (NAFTA) that was reached as far back as nineteen ninety-four (1994) and the Trans Pacific Free Trade Deal brokered by former President Barack Obama in the year two thousand and twelve with a block of twelve nations from the countries in Asia. When this is done, stage will now be set for greater exploits and challenges and we can be sure of winning and protecting our economy for the future.

Look China is stepping up efforts in trying to become the next leader of free trade and to my surprise; I am seeing many governments and nations trying to join them. This is a planned deception, do you know why, the Chinese have the most nationalist and monopolistic economy in the world where majority of the banks are operated by the government from telecommunications, to manufacturing and technology.

The adventure for free trade is aimed at helping to export more to other countries in the world. Whiles back home in China foreign companies are restricted in their operations. A foreign company can only setup a joint venture with a Chinese company when that company wants to operate in China. Will this country's free trade mutually benefit all the parties involved? Think about it yourself.

After the withdrawal of the country from all free trade deals, the government should now work on the plan of creating a standardized single policy that will govern internal and international trade policy respectively. The department of commerce as the law enforcement agency of the government can then work on implementing tariff amount on all products that cross our borders into our country.

This will be very easy to implement because the department of commerce already has a lot of these products listed at their website. A little research revealed that there are about twenty thousand product categories listed at the department of commerce. The department of commerce should impose tariffs on those products we don't need so much.

Building on the history of our country by looking back at the times of the First World War and the Second World War respectively, we can understand that there are some equipment's or machinery that our country will absolutely depend on other countries for supplies. Such commodities can be exempted from the tariff code so that our country doesn't suffer the country will balance out on that issue.

For example, when you visit every government office, business office, factories and other places, almost all the computers in those offices are made in either China or one of the Asian countries. The government can also include high technology current generation components that are used in warplanes, guided missiles and maybe aircraft carriers. Such products or components can be exempted when implementing the tariff code.

Chapter 16

The Government Should Introduce Subsidies to support American Companies

The meaning of the English word subsidy is a grant paid by a government to an enterprise that benefits the public such as a petroleum refinery company or an energy generating company. For example, the word subsidy can be used like for research in financing artificial intelligence research. The government can therefore decide to embark on a program of subsidizing critical sectors with of the economy so that the cost will not be solely on the company's that operates in our homeland.

The strategic transformation of the United States of America into an industrial powerhouse of the world started with the administration of former President George Washington in the eighteen hundred (1800's). The greatest work was done by the strategic treasury secret Alexander Hamilton when he together with his team outlined the strategic document that will make America an industrialized country for the world. And when the government of George Washington embarked on the policy of enforcing the measures stated by the treasury secretary. The country emerged strongly from nothingness and became the economic zone of the world. The country toppled and surpassed Britain and Germany to become the most industrialized country in the world. This status we have gradually lost and we are now trailing behind China and India is fast closing the gap.

One of the key factors that helped the American industrial sector was the government subsidy initiative that helped other countries to survive the economic pressure and cost of production is the availability of government subsidy. Now, as part of Alexander Hamilton strategic plan for the industrialization of the United States of America, he proposed that the government should introduced subsidy for the critical sectors of the economy. When the subsidies are properly implemented, the government will then directly compliment the efforts of companies and the help them by paying part of their bills.

These measures will reduce the pressure on company's expenditure thereby encouraging more companies to invest in the country. Indeed, with the high subsidies that the government started giving to companies, many companies from Britain moved to site their companies in the United States of America. Till date, the United Kingdom is the country that has invested more in the United States by setting up factories and companies in the United State of America.

Although the subsidy package of the United States government was going to cost the country several billions of dollars. Yet the government made the policy a reality and many companies emerged on our lands. The government started subsidizing essential and critical industries of our country like exploration of crude and natural gas, the health sector subsidy and the energy sector.

The aerospace sector, the defense sector and the automobile sectors all benefitted from government subsidy. By the year nineteen seventy-nine (1979) the administration of former President Ronald Reagan withdrew many of the subsidies and authorized waivers to the state department to buy things from outside the United State of America. This decision of the president will be the greatest and costly mistake in the history of this country.

Around the early nineteen eighties (1980's) the leaders of the communist republic of China met in Beijing to discuss key policies that will help them to transform China into the industry power house of the World. Many issues were discussed and the government agreed to pay subsidies to both local and international companies that will invest in their country. The Chinese government drafted adequate policies and then created industrial cities and later gave the invitation to foreign companies to invest in China. The Chinese government is paying out heavy subsidies to foreign and local companies that invest in China. And guess what, many companies have been attracted to China at the expense of the United States. In less than three decades,

on the lines of our national development, after so many years of economic transformation and successful achievement, the government felt that the country has become successful enough and some of the subsidies were withdrawn leaving all the cost on the shoulders of the companies operating in the country. This event will later spell doom for the country when China stepped up unto the world stage. China has rapidly transformed into one of the most industrialized country of the world beating the United States of America in terms of industrial output and production.

The miserable story about the future of America is that, the government is even contemplating of withdrawing funding for the import and export bank. This bank had actually played vital roles in the stabilization of the country's export competitiveness at the world stage.

The time is now and government should vigorously overhaul the system. If good policies are practiced, the economy will gradually return to the path of sustainable development. It is going to be difficult for the government though but with strong determination the country will overcome all obstacles and return to the path of growth and prosperity.

The government should come to the reality that the only way to maintain the competitiveness of the country in the world today is to introduce subsidies. It was American industrialization principles that promoted the country to success. Now, the new leaders of our great country have become confused and therefore have neglected the fundamental principles of the country's success and we are now pursuing policies that make it continually difficult for the country to handle.

Look, countries like China, Japan and South Korea among other countries have all followed the American industrialization principles and here we have them competing strongly against the United States of America. For example, when the Asian countries were following their own trade policies none of those countries became a world superpower, but shortly after they have followed the American industrialization principles drafted by Alexander Hamilton and former President George Washington, those countries have emerged so strongly that America depends on them for the very things we once produce here.

The government should re-implement and reinstate the subsidy. This will reduce the cost of investing in the United States of America. When this happens, it will become very simple for some companies to move production from overseas countries back to the United States. Many countries that moved to China and other parts of the World as a result of the subsidies and other attractive packages that those countries have implemented to attract foreign companies there are now creating problems to the companies.

For example, an American company producing products in China will now have to wait long hours to get their products from their suppliers. The cost of shipping or freight and the cost of inventory and the hidden cost of damaged products during transit all point to the difficulties our companies are currently facing out there as a result of moving to those places without fully accessing the cost. The government should intervene by restoring the subsidies.

Chapter 17

The Government Should Reinstate Pecuniary Bounties.

When we talk about pecuniary bounties we are pointing to the government paying out direct subsidies to private firms in a capitalist economy. The issue of the role of government in reviving the manufacturing sector of the United States took a center stage in the administration of former President Barack Obama and George Bush. They tried aggressively to consider whether the introduction of pecuniary bounties will help them to revive the manufacturing sector of the United States.

Although this topic was fiercely debated yet both Congress and government did not enforcement it as a law and therefore, the good benefits identified with pecuniary bounties remain in the good books of America and yet our local companies and firms are struggling to survive.

On the fifth day of December, seventeen ninety-one (1791) the former treasury secretary by name Alexander Hamilton working with former president George Washington suggested that the manufacturing sector will be key to the rise of the United States of America. He therefore proposed that since the economy was very young around that time, the government should implement a policy that will allow privately owned companies operating in the United States to receive pecuniary bounties periodically as they operate in the country.

The country actually implemented the strategy of former treasury secretary Alexander Hamilton, Congress and the government of former President George Washington implemented them and many companies moved to operate in the United States of America.

Along the line, after the country emerged as the most industrialized country in the world, many of the American leaders easily lost sight of the fundamental pillars that have brought the United States to world stage. The government of former president Jefferson and the Democratic and Republican Congress opposed the use of pecuniary bounties.

Again, the administration of former President Madison, and the Congress of his time also opposed the position of the government paying pecuniary bounties or subsidies to firm's operating in the United States of America. The decision of these leaders will later lead to the downfall of America in the years to come. Our country presently needs transformation so that the cost of running a company in the country will be much easier.

Let me tell you something, almost all the most industrialized countries with the exception of the United Kingdom have all learnt from the American principles of industrialization. Countries like Germany and Japan focused their economies on the path of the United States and in a short period of time, they have emerged among the most industrial superpowers of the world.

These countries did not do anything strange to transform and their economies, they simply adopted what the United States was doing and they tried to do it well. They are now having industrial output that surpasses that of the United States of America. A country like Japan has become so rich to the extent that they are now one of the largest holders of the United States of America treasury notes or sovereign debt.

When the Chinese also met in (1989) to discuss the key factors that will help them to transform their economy. They look and examined the principles of industrialization by the American government proposed by Alexander Hamilton. They adopted some of the factors and even modified them. They introduced their own policies that will help them to become industrialized in the world.

You will be surprised to know that as a result of determination and carefulness, China has now emerged as the largest manufacturing country in the world. This is just about a period of three decades. In less than one single generation, China has transitioned from nothingness to become the largest and most industrialized country in the world. The number of cars produced in China in (2016) is so huge that the United States does not come anywhere near them.

Do you know how the Chinese managed to emerge at the world stage? They adopted the principles of industrialization once operated by the United States of America. After they have adopted the policies, they created well organized industrial hubs and cities that will make it easy for various companies to manufacture and produce large quantities of products in the same city. After doing this, they invested heavily in educational system that surpasses that of the United States of America.

Surprisingly, when the Chinese have finished putting these initiatives in place, they invited foreign companies to invest in their country. The Chinese government has also created a credit facility that makes it possible for local Chinese to get access to money. As a result of this, there are several hundreds of thousands of companies owned and operated by Chinese. This is a practice that Alexander Hamilton proposed and was successful in America here for over two hundred years.

The Chinese government offer incentives to foreign companies and locals who invest their monies in the manufacturing sector. The Chinese government is giving pecuniary bounties to all privately held companies operating in the manufacturing sector of China.

Currently, the Chinese governments pays bounties to firms and even offer other incentives like paying light bills, water bills and sometimes the cost of transportation for the company's. These measures adopted by the Chinese government have actually made it possible for Chinese firms to produce goods at relatively cheaper prices that strangle life out of American firms. The United States now looks stranded as the Chinese are aggressively scuffling all the efforts of the United States of America. In fact, it looks like the Chinese want to capitalize on the inactions of American leaders to break up the American economy.

Governments all over the world have found that one of the most powerful ways to encourage manufacturing in a country is to pay pecuniary bounties to firms that operate in the designated country. As I have said earlier, the government of the United States of America has practiced these policies for almost two centuries and it has worked well for our country. Bounties can serve as a source of positive encouragement as companies can direct rely on the help of the government to produce goods and products at relatively reasonable prices.

Look I can confidently tell you that, it has been established that these bounties have the tendency to stimulate and drive the formation of new enterprises in an economy. A typical example is the case of China where more than one million factories have been established in less than three decades. These bounties can increase the chances of companies making more profits whiles reducing or entirely diminishing the risks of companies making losses in their operations.

Finally, when pecuniary bounties are paid to privately operated firms, the advantage is that the companies in the sector that are receiving the bounties can produce products or goods that sells cheaper than products from other countries that do not have such policies. So, I would advocated that the American government should bring back the pecuniary bounties so that our firms will not be directly exposed to cash shocks and other factors that have caused many American companies to register for bankruptcy. If someone tells you that the American government cannot reintroduce these bounties, then look at China.

Chapter 18

The Government Should Encourage New Inventions And Discoveries.

There have been several inventions and discoveries by many generations of humanity. During the time of the Greek empire, there were wonderful inventions and discoveries in the field of Science, Mathematics and Philosophy among other things. It will interest you to know that several years after the Greek empire; our educational systems are still making reference to the inventions and discovery that were propounded by the Greeks.

The Roman Empire also brought with it wonderful inventions in the field of sciences, Mathematics and technology. We are still using some of the inventions and discoveries from the era of the Roman Empire. A typical example of one of the Roman Empire inventions in use today is the calendar or the Gregorian calendar. The whole world is now being controlled by the inventions of the Roman Empire.

This has been the fundamental for the success of many countries in the world from the era of Empire to the era of nations. Every country or nation encourages its people to invent or discover things. So, when you read, the history of the nation's, you will realize that several people have made contributions in the fields of science, engineering, mathematics and language arts to brings humanity to the level where we have gotten to now. At every point in times, the world needs inventors and discoveries that will make the systems of the World better and then make the world a better place to live. This is the nature of the world and when Americans brought out the best in them we entered into the great era of our nation.

Though the government created a convenient environment for the invention and discoveries of materials in this country, the country emerged to become one of the most in the powerful nations in the world for several years. We can mention the inventions of airplanes, automobile, advance machineries, aircraft carriers and other wonderful things that were invented in this country. The greatness of America was by large sustained by the coordination that exists among the system of the United States of America.

However, the United States of America will not be able to invent or discover everything. This now brings us to the point where we will have to encourage our home-grown talents to invent and discover more things in the field of science, technology and arts. Then, in the places where we are not able to invent, we should create adequate and convenient environment that will attract other inventions or discoveries of other nations into our country. This has been a place where America has occupied with excellence.

The country has opened its doors very wide to invite and integrate foreign inventions into the systems of the world. The diversity of the United States has made it a wonderful country in the world. The nation is sometimes called the land of opportunity as many people are given the opportunity to serve the nation in any capacity that will benefit the nation and humanity at large.

Previously, the United States of America was very dominant as the country where many patents were once created or developed, but due to several budgetary cuts of the government that affect the educational systems of the United States of Americas, Japan has overtaken the United States to the first position as the place where more discoveries and inventions are made. Whiles Japan has moved to first position, the United States has fallen to the second position and China has suddenly risen to the third position as the place where more inventions and discoveries are made in the world. So, the United States of America should encourage the use of such inventions and discoveries that have been made in other countries more particularly those which pertains or relate to various equipment's or machinery.

So, when the government of the United States of America allows or encourage the integration of foreign inventions into our country, this will help our country to complement our weaknesses by using the successful inventions of other economies. This policy by government will be the most useful and unquestionable assistance that can be given to manufacturers in our country.

It's is sometimes dangerous to integrate the technology or machineries of other countries into the key sectors of our economy, but it has been proven that, the benefits of integrating foreign inventions or machinery exceeds the disadvantages. We should therefore encourage the government and companies to constantly adopt foreign inventions and discoveries so that our country does not lag behind other countries.

The government of our nation should encourage our local companies and industries to invent and discover more new inventions in the field of technology or machinery. We must make judicious efforts to improve upon the systems of our economy. Whiles we are working to improve the older system; we should also work to invent new things in the future. We must busily and actively contribute to the development of the World just as America has been known to be in the past.

One of the ways the government can invite other countries to bring their inventions and discoveries to America is to introduce pecuniary rewards that will allow foreign companies to enter the American market without paying huge border crossing taxes. Again, the government can allow foreign firms to bring their inventions to the United States by retaining their exclusive privileges as the inventors of the intellectual property. The government should also implement a task force that will monitor the utility of invention, or discovery in all the sectors of our economy. And fortunately, the laws of the United States have been made to allow for the efficient use of inventions and discoveries in this country.

It is a common thing to see the most industrialized nations sometimes placing embargo on the export of critical technology or inventions.

Previously, Intel used to be the main supplier of processors chips to the Chinese government. Along the line, the United States government accused China of using the supercomputer to test nuclear weapons and has banned the export of supercomputer chips to China.

This is sometimes one of the critical challenges government and corporations face when they attempt to attract other inventors of critical machinery or machines. This will actually not help the development of the world and therefore government should overcome their differences so that the best state of the art machinery and technologies can be used everywhere in the world to make the systems of government across the nation's more efficient than it is now.

The United States has actually done well in this regard and can be congratulated severally for the wonderful work that has been done. We should encourage the use of both local and foreign inventions in this country. Prohibition of any kind will only prevent the supply and use of technology and this will not help any country. We have gotten to a point where there should be more cooperation amongst nations in the fields of science and technology. And I believe that if government will do well, the benefits will overcome the disadvantages that will be recorded as a result of these policies the government pursing.

Chapter 19

The American Desire For Change

When you embark on an excursion to the industrial cities of the United States like Michigan during the Christmas vacation plainly sums the story of how Donald Trump won the electoral college votes on his way to becoming the president of America. I believe that he won the elections because of the so many closed down factory buildings that are not operational in the cities and towns of this great nation. The United States was a successful protectionist economy and what I mean is that protectionism actually built America and gave her the power of global imperialism. So, to turning down protectionism for free trade and globalization is to fundamentally reject the very pillars that have sustained the economic success of the United States.

The United States is currently heading towards a potential collapse as our industry or manufacturing sector has declined drastically. We cannot afford to sit down unconcerned to see the worse calamity befall this country. We need to do well from the government to our politicians and then down to the economic planners and advisers. The country needs to urgently adapt to new policies that will help the government to keep the national debt at sustainable levels.

The moment our government abandoned protectionism right here in the United States and willingly entered into several free trade agreements, our country now find herself in a situation where she is directly competing with low wage countries for local and international markets. The United States of America finds herself in a miserable situation that has resulted in many companies and factories moving offshore to invest in low wage countries. The end results of this economic situation can be clearly seen in the number of closed down factory buildings that are seen everywhere in America today. For example, the aviation sector cannot build an airplane without parts from China. The nation cannot independently build warships, aircraft carriers and even sophisticated missiles without having to depend on parts imported from China. This country has severally made it clear that they are not concerned about America and can easily shutdown or cut supplies to the United States now that our dependence on the Chinese made goods and machinery has increased.

Look at this pitiful development that has emerged in the consumer sector of the economy. Almost every day, the leading retail stores operating across the length and breadth of this nation ends up transferring large sums of billions of dollars to China, Vietnam, Mexico, India, Taiwan, South Korea, Singapore, Philippines and Malaysia and other low wage nations to pay for the goods bought by American consumers. This is the exact opposite of what it used to be a few decades ago, the tables have flipped within a short time and the government should adopt new strategies urgently to curtail this worrisome economic situation.

Currently it is true that we get cheap goods, equipment, machinery and foods from these countries and they get our money in return. The government now spends billions of dollars over six hundred billion dollars annually to pay for the bills of imported goods. Monies that should have been invested in this country now find its way out of the country. The present economic situation will one day lead to a situation where the government may not have enough to even spend on basic necessities in the years to come. These countries are actually getting our money and by relationship it means that our wealth is now being transferred to these low wage countries.

Because the money we pay to this country is actually in dollars, these monies will be returned back to the United States of America here. Do you know how it will happen; these companies will come and pour out their dollars into our country by buying large companies and buildings that Americans are no longer able to manage. This is a flourishing trend and you can easily help yourself by looking at the electronic, semiconductor, furniture and clothing sectors of American industry. Everything is now made outside the United States and we are seeing foreigners taking over massive wealth and assets in this country.

During the days of the presidency of former President Ronald Reagan, the United States had strong tariffs and the economy was booming. Around the same time about a quarter of the working people were actively engaged in manufacturing. According to the records, the United States served as the single largest creditor nation in the world. This means that around this time, many countries in the world owed the United States several billions of dollars usually for importing finished goods from America.

America is currently the largest debtor nation in the world in less than three decades as a result of liberal political choices of the various administrations of governments towards free trade. Moreover, before the administration of Ronald Reagan, the United States was the largest exporter of finished goods. America was also the largest single importer of raw materials that were necessary to make these finished goods.

Presently, things have actually changed and swayed from the reach of Americans and we don't know what to do now in other to salvage the situation. The United States has now become the largest importer of finished goods and in contrast has become one of the key exporters of raw materials like iron ore, oil or fuel, coal, timber, that are now used to assemble the materials in China which are later imported back into this country.

Protectionism built America and this was not the first time that these protectionist economic ideologies were practiced.

The British also practiced protectionism and everything around business was structured to favor the manufacturing sector of Great Britain. The British government of that time emulated the successful economic principles of the Dutch. When they researched about it, it was proven that the Roman and the Greeks all practiced protectionism to high levels of economic successes. We have outlined some of the strategies that both government and citizens can use to revamp the industry sector of the United States of America.

Other Books By The Same Author

Do you need additional books from this author, then you are at the right place, please check out these books on amazon:

The Apocalypse Of Great America

The Economic Super Power